# WHAT CAN I SEE?

# BEACH

ticktock

| Northamptonshire Libraries & Information Service | |
| --- | --- |
| 80 002 580 398 | |
| Peters | 16-Mar-06 |
| 551.46 | £4.99 |
| | |

Copyright © **ticktock Entertainment Ltd 2006**
First published in Great Britain in 2006 by ticktock Media Ltd.,
Unit 2, Orchard Business Centre, North Farm Road, Tunbridge Wells, Kent TN2 3XF

ISBN 1 86007 852 4
Printed in China

**Picture credits**
t=top, b=bottom, c=centre, l=left, r=right
Ardea images: 3b, 7t. FLPA: 4-5, 9c, 13c, 14-15c, 18bl, 19c, 2021c.
Every effort has been made to trace the copyright holders, and we apologise in advance for any unintentional omissions.
We would be pleased to insert the appropriate acknowledgements in any subsequent edition of this publication.

A CIP catalogue record for this book is available from the British Library.

# contents

# At the beach

There is so much to see on the beach – from birds soaring high in the sky to creatures lurking in rock pools and animals scurrying over the sand.

# What can you see at the beach?

Crab

Seaweed

Seagull

Puffin

Starfish

Boats

Limpets

Seal

Driftwood

 **crab**

Crabs have a hard shell which **protects** their soft bodies. There are about 4,500 different kinds of crab.

Crabs have 10 legs for swimming and walking. They can only walk sideways!

Strong **pincers**
on the crab's front
legs are used to catch food.

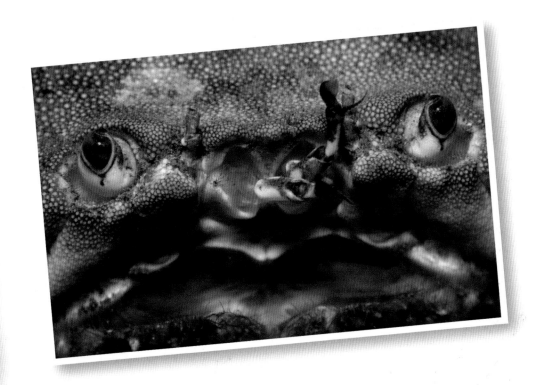

Some crabs are really small, but the
largest can be up to 3.6 metres wide.

#  seaweed

**S**eaweed is a type of plant that grows in the ocean. It is found mainly in **shallow** water because it needs sunlight to survive.

Everything seaweed needs to grow is in the seawater.

There may be up to 6,000 types of seaweed. Some of them are dull but others are beautiful.

Seaweed is a good food for people
as well as animals.

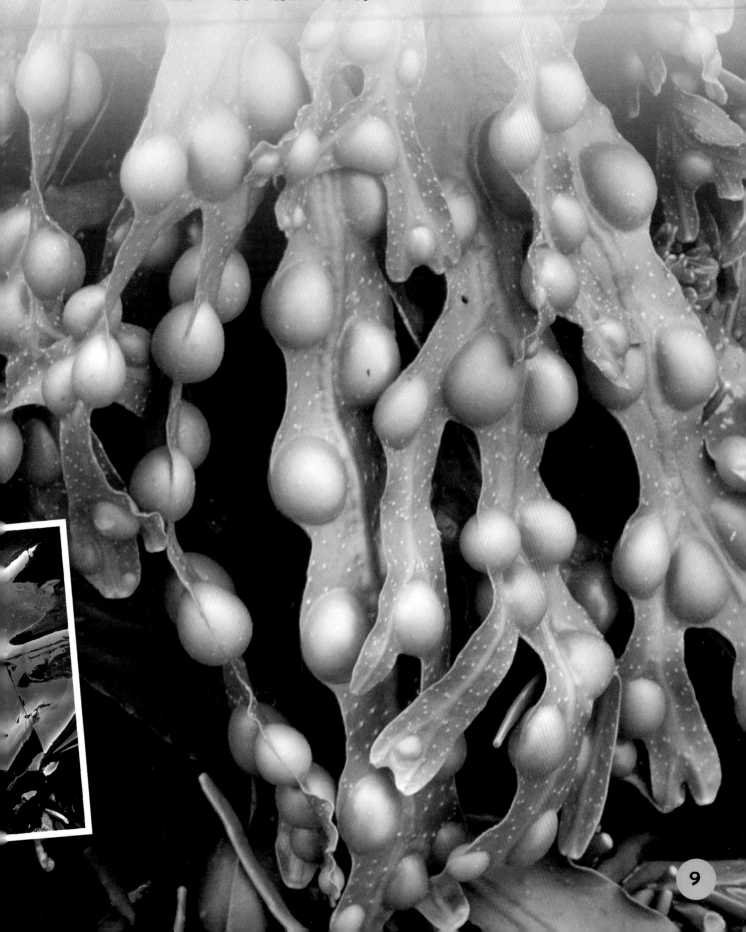

# seagull

**S**eagulls are large, noisy birds with powerful wings. They are found on the coast all over the world.

Seagulls build their nests on the edge of cliffs. They usually live in large groups.

Seagulls have sharp beaks, which help them to eat fish.

**Flocks** of gulls fly around searching for food.

The long, **narrow** wings of the seagull help it to glide fast over the waves.

**P**uffins are easy to recognize because of their black and white **plumage.**

They have brightly coloured **triangular** bills and orange legs.

Puffins are good swimmers. They dive deep under the water to catch the fish they like to eat.

Puffins use their wings for flying and swimming.

13

# starfish

**S**tarfish live in the ocean along rocky coasts. Sometimes they can be found washed up on the sand.

Starfish arms are strong enough to open the **shellfish** they eat.

The mouth of
a starfish is
in the middle
of its body.

**Mouth**

**Suckers**

Underneath the
starfish are **suckers** that
help it to cling to rocks.

**M**any types of boat are found along the coastline. Some are used for fun, and others for work.

Small boats can be used for fishing near the coast.

Some fishing boats can go out in deep water. They use nets to catch fish.

Lifeboats are specially
built so they are
difficult to sink.
They can go out
in rough sea to
rescue people.

 # Limpets

Limpets have pointed shells and are found on rocky shores.

Limpets eat **algae** and other ocean plants like seaweed.

Limpets have only one foot, which **ripples** to move it along. They have **tentacles** that they use to feel.

When they are not feeding, limpets fix themselves to a rock.

# seal

**S**eals are **mammals** that live in the sea. Some kinds of seal never leave the water, but others come to land to breed.

Seals have **flippers** that help them to move fast through the water.

Seals come up to the surface of the water to breathe through their **nostrils.**

Seals have thick **waterproof** fur. An adult seal may have 800 million hairs on its body.

A seal's body is covered with thick fat called blubber. This helps to keep the seal warm.

**D**riftwood is the name for wood that drifts around in the sea. It may be in the water for many years before it is washed to the shore.

Driftwood may come from wrecked ships, or from trees that were carried away by the ocean.

Artists often use driftwood to make **sculptures**.

Driftwood may have
travelled thousands of miles
before the waves carry it to the shore.

# Glossary

**Algae** Tiny plants that float in the water and are eaten by sea creatures

**Flippers** Flat limbs on the side of an animal's body that help it to swim

**Flock** A large group of birds

**Mammal** An animal that breathes air and usually gives birth to live babies

**Narrow** Something with a thin width

**Nostrils** Holes in the nose or on the front of the head which an animal uses to breathe

**Plumage** The feathers of a bird

**Protected** Kept safe from harm

**Pincer** A type of claw with two parts that move together, a bit like a finger and thumb

**Ripples** To move with a wave-like motion

**Sculpture** A piece of art made by carving wood or stone

**Shallow** Not deep

**Shellfish** Ocean creatures with soft bodies that are protected by shells

**Suckers** Round-shaped objects that cling to other things by sucking

**Tentacles** Thin, flexible arms that are used for feeling or holding

**Triangular** Shaped like a triangle

**Waterproof** Able to keep out water